MOSS

MOSS

poems

Joey Berger

Clare Songbirds
Publishing House

Clare Songbirds Publishing House Poetry Series
ISBN 978-1-957221-21-2
Clare Songbirds Publishing House
Moss © 2025 Joey Berger

Printed in the United States of America
FIRST EDITION

140 Cottage Street
Auburn, New York 13021
www.claresongbirdspub.com

I would firstly like to acknowledge the love and support of my family — my parents, Bonnie and Sam, and my sister, Haley. This book would not have been possible without them. They have taught me to always live by the ideals of humility, curiosity, and above all, kindness. I would also like to thank all of my extended family, friends, teachers, and mentors throughout the years who continue to inspire and uplift me. Finally, I would like to thank Clare Songbirds Publishing House for taking a chance on me and helping publish my first book of poems.

"I write for the still-fragmented parts in me, trying to bring them together. Whoever can read and use any of this, I write for them as well."
— *Adrienne Rich*

Contents

Rainy Mornings

The teardrops follow me in perpetuity,
Aimlessly drifting across the car windows
With the grace of a black swan and the control of a teenage driver.
Nameless and faceless,
They drive their own fantasies and satisfy their urges
To let go and lose themselves—
How pitiful we must seem in comparison.

I am only as beautiful as my face,
Yet these mornings dissolve the facets of my imagination
Begging to corrupt my already infantile soul—
The jokes on them: I don't have one.
Oh, how I swaddle myself in the blankets of mediocrity
That these rainstorms can so effortlessly wash away.
What more I can do I don't know.

Someone remarks on the rain's sorrow.
They don't understand—
They will never understand.
What daisies I surround myself with
Continues to amaze me, their vapid existences
Draining all thought and essence out of their convicts—
Those gentle, wavering flames threatened by something as weak as the wind.

But the rain brings such a wonderful aftermath!
The crisp, niche scent that derives from the soaked grass and flowers,
Which are irrevocably dense in their looming lives.
Fiddled by the sun and cement,
The rain, convoluted in its truth,
Becomes nothing and is quickly forgotten—
It lacks only the tiniest element: teeth.

Why so feeble the rain is, I don't know.
The weightless figments of my imagination
Can only aim to profit off of the only time I can spend with the rain—
Those damp, calculating mornings
That adults despise and children exploit seem so insignificant,
And maybe they are,
But with the inductions of the droplets, a new world becomes.

Chai

It frightens me, how much I know.
Set on a patterned rug with stains and tears,
My eyes inevitably lose all control,
Wished into a haze of novelty.

In a plump high-top chair,
Those surrounding me fill the air with contempt
And hot air, regardless of the cool breeze seeping in.
A beacon of flavor in a sea of flushed cheeks,

Sweetened with cinnamon grains and rich culture,
My cup of chai takes the upper hand in
Purifying the forces working against harmony.
Almost sickeningly sweet, but always there.

The smile of my silver spoon soothes me—
Reflections of light and thrush bounce off
The meek walls of this cobblestone cafe,
With no end in sight or in mind.

Loud voices and dirty thoughts nevertheless fill the air,
Caught in a breeze of infidelity.
On the crooked, baroque table, the light, creamy elixir
Satisfies my own infidelities.

The window across from me tints my perceptions
And crows the oblique lens that ongoing whispers admire.
What a sweet, sweet world we live in—
One where every glance is returned by a glare.

It must be overwhelming,
The burdens of society that threaten the balance
Between nature and chaos, beauty and insanity.
But oh, another day will pass.

Swiss Summers

The sunsets can only blind me once a month.
Sitting quietly on a field of incandescence,
Wildflowers accept the false promise of motion
And confine themselves to shattered curiosity—
Yet they illustrate the finest qualities of nature:
Emitting fumes that are utterly intoxicating and
Brightening the wings of butterflies—
I am certain that I found heaven.

Sipping from the cup of placid nectar,
Ibex and little red foxes survive on ecstasy
Rather than fear.
The lakes—glorious ponds of unwritten literature
Annihilate my only regrets.
Translucent in their souls, I can see right through them
Only to find that I can really see nothing.

Emptiness outweighs the passion that these spherical blue poppies
Laugh and put out in waves—
They are the only things keeping me going.
Their reflections are so meaningless and deceitful,
Resenting our mobility and refusing us knowledge.
What I can do in this place amazes me
And brings me only maladies of the heart, impossible to cure.

Golden villages upon a hill look up at the spires of snow,
The spires majestic in their appearance and frigid in their contentions.
Medieval people, content with bread and cheese,
Lose nothing in their daily prophecies of enchantment.
I am seduced by the pointy chalets that survive in a symbiotic relationship
With the trees, birds, and worms that leech onto their skin.
Her heart is here, in the Swiss mountains.

Ringing from door to door,
The authentic bells of Swiss beauty find themselves
On such peaceful creatures as cows!
I wish I can be a cow in my next life,
Resuscitated into the speckled beast that eats and sleeps,
And lives without fault.
A Swiss cow, my God!

Please don't forget me because I promise I won't forget you.
Licking my panna ice cream on the elusive beaches
Of an electric blue lake,
Children giggle and are hushed under the sun.
I envy those who walk down the streets,
Armed with the most dangerous weapons: chocolate and choux à la crème.
How pitiful that my visit is only short-term.

Hugged by the illustrious blossoms of hearthstones,
I open up to what faith remains in me.
What preceded seems like a toad, insignificant and warty
In all swamps of zealous behavior.
From the blossom's ashes I arise,
A duplicitous savant of clarity—
Milked and managed.

The new year settles in,
Which makes my departure even more disheartening.
What remains is a desire to return forever,
To return to the lack of longing and swaddled disposition.
Faceless and primitive in their nature,
The pine trees of the forest bristle their cones to stain me with
An unforgettable grip.

The Queen's Hamlet

In a fertile, open plot of land lies a village
Ridden with the burdens of peasants,
Filled with the presence of a queen.

The cornucopia of this haven,
A small pond of fresh country,
Is stained with swans and tears.

An icebox encapsulated with contention
She leaves behind, desperate to escape
Her tailored dresses and idyllically soft cakes.

And for what?
Why a playhouse embroidered with the works
Of a farmer, of course.

Simple gardens of squash and romaine lettuce stand proud,
Nurtured by the queen herself, given that she is not
Plagued by her flawed perfection or out in her rowboat.

Little rabbits and goats and pigs run-afoot,
Duplicitous in their sunny displeasure that only she,
Their landlady Marie Antoinette, can sympathize with.

Flitting and fluttering about are the swans,
Elegantly marking the water with their black feet
And unnerving calm.

What luminescent locks of hair she has!
What splendid raspberry macarons she devours!
What great sadness consumes her!

The straw roofs, alive with splendor among the
Cobblestone huts and wooden balconies, can only
Keep the queen content for so long.

Her farm is her court, and her chickens are her love.
Tomorrow she will swim,
Plunge into the depths of her psyche that sully her porcelain skin.

Falling

Indispensable, the buoy shakes about,
Grasping at unidentifiable straws.
I promised myself another chance—
Heavy and dense the water sits.

What I lack is touch and feeling:
I don't feel depressed, but empty.
Depression seeps in much faster and noticeably,
But this thing I feel is a void.

Autumn Remorse

Slow and motionless,
The leaves address their fate,
Pushing towards my insignificant face
Under the grand sycamore tree.

Forced capitulation is inevitable—
Those thick souls
Sprinkling their bright, powdered grain
As intensely as a hummingbird flaps its wings.

Only the sick fascination with decay
They hold can overwhelm their innocence.
Stability is so fragile,
Fenced on the border of exasperation.

With the brisk, spiced air comes
An appropriation of romanticized glory.
Valid in its efforts,
The truth lies in the thick, thick mud.

Mélusine

Plip pop, plip pop.
The light visible is weak,
Courtesy of a full moon.

The cobblestones confine
The splendor. What approaches
Is a voice of grace that

Provides a song full of promises
To end all drunken ends—
Friends, I can only

Believe so much.
The muddled water,
Too unfamiliar for fishermen,

Is crystal clear to me. O great depths—
Those shapes that come near me.
I try to rise above,

Float in the air that only fish see.
I miss what sick song
Formerly filled my ears. At the forefront

Of this icy bay, a moat maddens,
Infiltrating the harmony
Of the natural onus.

Pumpkin in the Orchard

Only such a thing as a bumblebee could be seen,
Blessed by the futile shadow of its rooted counterparts.
A nasal aroma lay among the orchard,
Thick and accentuated by the decay of fresh Gala apples.

Under the tallest apple tree lay the most peculiar thing: a pumpkin.
Not even a traditional, boring orange pumpkin
Plastered with a gritty smile carved from its guts.
Infatuation plagued this demure pumpkin.

Sanguine in its efforts, this pilgrim exerted influence over its body,
A blatant yet familiar milky-white sack of bones.
Hush-hush, crows recognized its malevolence
And turned to brighter pastures.

This forlorn pumpkin, lonely and resentful,
Found itself in quite the dilemma.
Grounded, it was just a pumpkin,
A victim of the orchard's tainted gaze.

Broken Pictures

Nostalgia lies up at night in my mind,
Desperate to escape and become reality,
Yet ever confined to the chains of my brain.

Chocolate ice cream on the beach,
Spring hikes in the forests,
Plucking bright yellow dandelions from the lawn.

The chicken inside clucks out
Only to be muted by its own voice—
A supernatural cluck of intrigue.

What world I once had is gone,
Ridden with worms and mushrooms,
Decomposed by the natural cycle,

The cycle that humanity perverts
And I resent.
The framework is golden,

Seared into all aspects of the room,
Contrasted by its hallowed halls
And emptiness.

Hope ferries me away,
Taking my past and
Manipulating it—

It was the best of times,
It was the worst of times,
But it was my time.

Woodwinds

A looming sound pollutes the air,
Waiting politely to serve in full form.
You're dusty and bony,
Happiest alone and mute. You

Lack the brightness, wrapped up in your own
Contentions. Ivory tusks of whining
Elephants—their own weapon is unsuspected mirth.
Up and down, backwards and forwards,

Your hands abet a beautiful disease,
Your mouth soaks the wooden puppet,
Your lungs gasp for more,
Your mind borders on insanity.

But it's so easy to get carried away
Flirting with the beast of beauty.
Your potion is more pungent than
Alice's but your foxhole remains. Insipid

Gold and brass melt to forge a sword
Of uncertainty and muddled merriment. Countered
By the oboe, clarinet, flute, English horn,
Order is restored but wavers.

Edged on by a first-class pencil,
Pointing sharply and erasing mistakes,
Music becomes math,
Where flaws become catastrophic.

Perfection is not one option:
It is the only option.
Failure squeaks so meekly yet noticeably.
That which once was so snug

Is impoverished, whittled down
By blank eyes that instinctively
Turn towards you—
The mediocre become masters. Audiences

Are the reasons you kill yourself every day.
The fleeting sublimity that
Releases the urges, jumpy as Mexican beans
That formerly closed in on

You. Forgiving and forgetting
Is the name of the game, my friend.
Soon you will be forgotten,
Your worries insignificant

And your existence non-existent.
A fawn in the headlights,
Awaiting the moonlit eve of destruction,
Reeds hop and hop—

Their last words: "We will be there."
They will not be there,
Thrusted into the elusive stark of
Their grim desires.

To last, to live upon the stage:
The glances become chances
In this cutthroat industry—
Wood insistently beckons.

The Groundhog In the Garden

Eats all the vegetables: spinach, tomatoes, leeks.
I am powerless without a rake in my hand or a rock at my feet.
He extracts love and nourishment
So that I am punished, pushed to the brink.
Compared to me, this groundhog is immortal and omniscient—
I walk through life step by step
While this fiend skitters without remorse:
Props to him.
What did they do wrong, the crops?
Grow too tall, shine too irresistibly?

I'm ashamed that I gave him a purpose,
Practically drove him to a life of crime.
Who am I to judge?
I fancy myself a Marshall in the court of pasta and cake,
But not in garden theft.
Oh, how frivolous it sounds to say!
Sitting on the porch every wispy, summer evening,
I read my book and write in my journal,
Not without looking out of the corner of my eye
For the hairy stump whose company I can't resist.

After the Rain

Without the rain, I would be nothing, and you would be nothing:
The supplements that would brighten our cool skin
Would be famine and drought.
It gave me a soul, I burgeoned out of it like a tulip opening its petals,
Sudden and complacent in my futility.

A cornucopia of nourishment sits upon Zeus's throne up in Mount Olympus,
Pondering when to grace us with its sticky presence—it does not realize that
It remains far after it believes. In plants, bodies, and souls,
We idly sit with a reverential disposition that softens our lies
As a tongue softens taffy.

Moss

I am soft and plump, a spongy peach of some sort, always bouncing back.
Left to my own devices, I become sick and lonely,
Forced to be some messed up measure of stability in nature.

So, so, so very supple are my grainy cheeks that easily pop like a bubble—
The bubble that is a paradox: a transparent mirage. I am not
A loser or a winner. I'm not anything. I'm just there,

Which sounds resentful, I know, but I do anything just to feel, even if it's anger.
The world certainly feels me, the cushion that points them in the right direction—
I am all but a rainbow: there to amuse, silently soaking in revelations.

Over and over, my emotions overwhelm me, planting seeds of deceit.
I don't want to be me anymore: bitter and dry, able to soak in everything
But myself. Desperate yet patient, I can only wait my turn.

I lay down on a lawn that continues to lose its green luster,
Shaped by everything it itself lays upon.
I can't understand its frail existence with all of its youth.

One flower drops a lavender petal—
No one seems to notice except for the yellowjacket drawn to its color,
Fulfilling for any creature in a ten-mile radius.

The shadow of a tree looms. It must reach over Canada, maybe even Greenland.
On the north-facing side of the tree lies my bandage of bondage,
Omnipresent across this forest of grandeur.

I see a great space of pewter light that calls me in to join for the long ride,
To infect it with my decadence that convolutes my existence.
I see my green skin. I must be dreaming—don't wake me up.

The Flower Show

I bite my tongue standing in the shadows of the orchids,
Watching with subtlety.
I think they're Indonesian or Colombian.

The other ongoing viewers push their way through,
Jabbing like a bunch of cockatoos. I am an island,
Standing by myself but not alone.

Banana flowers, birds of paradise, and bull thistle
Sweeten the air in tandem with one another,
Pollen floating like bubbles in the air.

I have allergies but my body doesn't encourage them.
The enclosed glass greenhouse teases me with its
Promise of open air.

Silly, silly, silly.
The flowers are drugs, some psychedelic aliments
That slowly corrode my mind.

I'm not afraid that I'll be happy,
But I am afraid that I won't get to choose to be happy,
Forever smiling in pain.

Paranoia has been slowly seeping in,
Poisoning the air by abetting toxic fumes—
It's their show, not mine, so why am I anxious?

I have moved along, and I can even see the door,
But my feet fail me, and I can't move,
Eyes glued to the exotic exodus of safety.

Gasping

How glorious—
My breaths uttered erratically.
My body screaming for oxygen,
Except for the already numb brain.

It feels nice to have that option,
To just live at your own will.
The air ushers me back in,
Soft and inviting.

Inertia

I wish I was a ball rolling down a hill indefinitely,
Living the life of recklessness like a motorcyclist
Zooming between cars on the highway.
Nothing would stop me—I would keep moving,

Free as a bird flying above the clouds.
Motion would follow me in perpetuity
Down the hill, picking up speed
As time goes on.

A force to reckon with,
I would be my own force,
With patience and orderliness
And superiority over all things inert.

Maybe I'd humor the fire in me
That's been frightened of charring everything
It touches. I wouldn't vie for attention
Even if I wanted it—

Contentment would be definite,
A condition of my loss of all self-control.
I would be an anomaly,
Defiant of physics and common sense.

It would be lonely,
Passing by nature with perfect clarity,
But never being able to stop and enjoy it.
I'd be moving, but I would always be moving.

I still retain confidence in my plan: I value
My happiness. Even though it's selfish,
I want to lose all feeling and have all my decisions made for me,
So I can drift away into my own world.

Washing My Hands

The best parts of my day are in the mundane things:
Watering my plants, salting my eggs, folding my clothes.
The sticky sap of the day's anxieties seem to disappear,
Pulled like a bad singer is hooked off the stage.

I can't help my constant sighs; they motivate me,
Reminding me of what reality looks like.
I'm sick and my grapes have mold,
But I at least have a chance for survival.

The ingenuity of the items around me is my parent,
Pushing me towards greatness. It's a strange strategy
As I always end up in my bed, alone and forlorn,
With my head on the pillow that I violently crave.

I lay in bed, and I stand in the shower, and I wash my hands
With the mandarin pine soap that gels and foams.
The only clouds I see each day are artificial, straight out of a
Dystopian novel.

The soap quietly reserves its apathy for the upcoming events,
But gradually accepts its fate. It is resentful and
I can't blame it. The sink showers the clouds with acid,
Extinguishing any existence it had.

I tend to leave my hand under the running water,
With water tracing my palm and the soap's aroma rushing to my nose.
But I can't leave it on for too long—it's only a matter of time
Before it washes me away.

The Black Cat's Figs

On the streets of Istanbul,
The mosques preside with their spires pointed up,
Preceded by the cobbled roads.

The affluent markets overrun by tourists and natives alike
Full of spices and lamb are conditional,
Managed by the highest degrees of intuition.

Cats, and only cats scurry about,
Hopping from roof to roof like some jumping spiders,
Testing the lengths of their nine lives.

Stretched thin and impoverished,
They somehow manage to make a scrappy living.
The wisest of them is the black cat,

Who basks in the sunlight atop
A carton of baroque figs, plump and ripe.
The bees and other cats don't dare take a bite.

The black cat retains little to no heat even in the sun
By way of the fountain only three feet away.
The figs are futile and cautionary,

But more importantly they are figureheads.
This cat is not wise and old or a revered veteran,
But a simple feline that lives in peace.

He drinks in the life of his living
In perfect clarity, a Sartre or Plato.
He is the opus.

A Christmas Morning

Is it for me, this present, and is it beautiful?
Oh my, is it fun and perfect and beautiful?

The red and green wrapping paper confound its entourage,
Blending blood and nature into a vicious weapon of deceit.

I know it's something special, it has to be.
My desires tempt me into making rash decisions and

Forcibly thrust me into the spotlight of my own dream.
The needles of the Christmas tree glisten in the hopeful sunlight

In the morning. Through the window, I see the other trees powdered
With snow, all dolled up for today.

Their opacity fascinates my trundle of a soul,
Placid and fragile in the wonder of the moment.

It is no time for the sun to act this ridiculous,
Abasing the green ribbons and white paper,

Fantastically arousing the jays and bluebirds into delirious song—
I think I hear Silver Bells, or is it Silent Night, or maybe just Christmas?

I can't remember anything they said, but I remember 179.
179, 179, 179.
God, why can't I comprehend?
He was in such a hurry and a tizzy,
Feeling entitled to make drastic claims
Just because he's in a lab coat
And has a PhD from Cambridge.
Who does he think he is,
Playing with guns in a protest,
Shoving lies down my throat
With intent.
I bet he wears that mask
To cover his ugly face
And conceal his garlicky breath.
But he said 179,
And I have to remember 179
So I must cut him some slack for now.

I'm on the border
Of Canada and the United States,
But customs is taking hours.
Sick to my stomach,
I want to cross
But realize it won't happen.
Maybe it's a good thing,
Me staying on the known side,
Even if that means mediocrity.
179, 179.
I slur when I try to speak it.
How can I understand something
That I can't even say?
Sin follows
And broods,
Accompanied by blackness,
A black that scares me
With its futile abominations.
A gift, a gift of desperation
Loves me
Until my heart stops.
But it still beats,
Beating as fast
As a fever overwhelms a child.

179.
I don't dare cry or scream,
Be some whiny brat.
I walk, walk, walk

Towards the light
But a voice calls me back.
It's the voice of my father,
But I quickly realize
That it's not
Because he just left an hour ago.

London Burning

The flame steps into oblivion.
I infuriate
Those who see me.

Yells are thrown around,
Utterly meaningless.
I fail

My others, my future.
I should run,
But there's no point.

Ruin
Is inevitable—
Forget it.

Parisian Cobblestone

Forging ahead,
Parisians roam the streets with intent,
Staining the streets with cigarettes.

The lively ruin of an imperfect city
Evinces a bittersweet despair
In tandem with irrevocable longing.

Qu'est-ce qui s'est passé?
Colonized by unquenchable thirst,
Grit fizzles out among the people,

Almost as fluid as the Seine itself,
Docked with swans and ducks
Curving between boats and tourists.

The streets are overcrowded with stores,
But the beauty of Haussmann apartments
Coupled with the aroma, prevail.

Paper boats in the Jardins du Luxembourg
Excite themselves,
Losing no movement or motivation with time.

The crêpe stands ripple with simplicity,
Yeomans of the French,
Crippled by temptation.

Jazz sings around the corner,
But it's not bright.
The fickle nature

Of the surroundings whisk
Away the enthusiasm
And turn Paris into a sweet city,

But lack understanding of its essence—
The prevalent conscience of a city,
A living, breathing thing.

Only the laughter of the air persists,
Tickling and hawing like a pig.
The hustle and bustle

Does not speak to the rich history,
Marked by artistic and literary culpability
Evident in daily life.

What seems to be an intricate place
Is much simpler than it really is.
It is a place of moderated pleasure

Where one can enjoy a pastry and coffee
While sitting at a cafe on the street,
Quietly reading a book without glamor.

The trees, scarce in number,
Cling on to this decadence
With scaly, warty arms

That somewhat enclose Paris,
Hiding what cannot be found:
The truth.

The Interview

I must ask, have you prepared?
Oh, that's a silly question, of course you haven't.
You don't wear
A solemn disposition, a tie, shiny loafers,
A glass chest or glass heart,

Maybe some sort of toupee?
Don't cry.
Why I only want to make sure
You are the perfect fit for our brand.
What's in your briefcase?

No, no? You can't open it?
What a pity,
Although I already sensed
It would be empty,
Some whole-hearted attempt to impress

Or rather repress me into submission.
Believe me, I want what's best for you.
Don't you agree?
I notice you look glum,
Cheer up boy. You are empty

But I can fix that,
Fill you with the sole of a shoe.
Do you like this one?
It's rough and dark,
But I find it to be quite fitting on you.

Let's try something else.
Your eyes look blank,
I have the key.
Glass eyes to match that empty head,
Oh, how perfect.

Don't feel overwhelmed,
You're sick now but in ten years
You will be grand.
I'm taking you on as my apprentice,
Aren't you lucky.

You'll be my soldier,
Prim and proper.
Your orders will be from me,
You'll learn the tricks of the trade.
Don't you agree? No, no? Well, that's a pity.

Double Entendre

Listen, listen, listen. No, you're not getting it.
I will be Bonnie and you will be Clyde,
And we will walk off in the sunset to our cave
Of jewels and ore deposits.
You might as well commit arson,
Because I am your home now.
None of this pleading and begging,
Why must you make this so hard?

The duplicity of the sun and moon above
Are distorting my words, those thieves.
Hear me now: I am.
Follow me into the light, you must,
Or else pigs will fly,
And that would be anarchy,
Which doesn't apply to us.
Isn't that right my friend?

Bring your sweatshirt and your brain,
We are surely going to need both.
These two most flaccid birds of a feather
Are our destiny. Lose this regret,
And join the group, be a team player.
Watch out for the stones,
They can be unforgiving when pressed.
That was a joke.

To ensure a peaceful trip,
Come up to the front of the car
And be my guide—lord knows I can't be my own guide.
The suckle I'm providing will give you ambrosia
And maybe a little amnesia, but that's all part of the plan.
You don't want to have to remember our escapades
Because then there won't be adventure in our new ones.
Now for the last time, will you join us?

Blueberrying in August

A sea of blueberries clouds my vision for miles on miles,
Blueberries frustrating the fields all around me.
The bees are sent into a tizzy, hypnotized by the sanguine color in sight,
A brightly sinister shade that infects what it can.
My measly straw basket is no match for the blueberries,
Extraordinarily plump and fresh,
Juicing into my mouth and onto my hand.
Maybe I'm in Maine or is it Michigan, I can't tell. Blueberries
Encumber my ability to separate reality from psychosis, love me until I'm sore.

Their glow refreshes me, placing me in a trance—
The blueberries that fall from the bushes plop onto the ground,
Sold at auction to the floor that constructs its own syrupy goodness.
Time is gradually sucked and wished away by the blueberries,
Obstructing the beach that I know awaits me on the other side.
I am so insignificant that the fields give up some amity
In the form of blueberries.
My feet feel invisible on the grass, harboring intimacy with the
Scraggly bushes hooked on the land in rows.

I relent in my urge to move forward so quickly—
Sensing my hesitance, the blueberries loosen their grasp,
Showing me the flowering blossoms atop the cliff on the seashore.
Slowly blueberries dissolve into clouds
Until I can no longer remember what possessed me.
I walk ahead and control myself,
Determined to enjoy the fruits of my labor.
The coast flashes like a bolt of lightning,
And before I know it, I am back in the fields surrounded by blueberries.

Among the Hyacinth

A grave appointment disrupts them,
Titillating with utter stasis.
The stars open up above
In a fickle sourness.

The finality is reprehensible,
Clearing the way for the discomfort
That trots about in lonely pastures,
Sowed by the fertile breath.

The hyacinth are passive,
Gradually vanishing in thickness
To consume the fields
In a deep flesh of home.

The Saboteur

Callous hearts in a void.
I await the stumbling decry
Of derision.

Caught in the glass ball,
How gratifying!
We connive together—The light

Debases the crook
I am.
Coercing the stasis,

A blue arc shadow—
Heavy heart, heavy mind;
A despot

Of eloquence.
Crumpled blackness
Rifts in a motionless foam.

Stabbed by an unrecognizable face
That wilts,
I crouch to level

This tor of subordination.
Erudite
Once I was,

And I gripped deep vines
Gratuitously—
Lifeless fingers, lifeless motives.

Something, someone
Lets me loose
Into a dark, dark sky.

The Sky and the Dogwood Tree

Blossoms blind me,
Fidgeting in the sky
So intent on making a splash.

To no avail,
Whispers shroud the wind,
Sealing a sanguine fate.

The bark is coarse—
Marbled and scaly,
The roots sit,

No opportunity to grow,
Although they do not wish it.
The pollen

Hides in the air,
Furiously ravaging
The sensitivity of my nature.

Enveloping the dogwood tree
Are bees,
Miles and miles of bees,

Suckling nectar fantastically.
The hive is not far,
Only a leap away,

Dashed in the shade
Of a thousand leaves.
The neurotic blue

Of the lachrymose atmosphere
Caresses the branches,
Milking it with mystery.

To only twist,
Live the natural life
Of apathetic acceptance.

Joey Berger is an undergraduate student at Yale University, studying English and Environmental Studies. He is originally from Briarcliff Manor, NY. His writing has been recognized by the Scholastic Art and Writing Awards, *The Post-Standard/Syracuse.com*, and Lifting Up Westchester. Joey is a staff reader for *The Yale Review, The Adroit Journal, The Yale Literary Magazine*, an editor for *The Environmentalist* at Yale, and an advocate for student journalism.

When he's not writing, he can be found exploring nature, reading at a coffee shop, or perusing through vintage clothing stores.